# Every Tiki has a

# SPIRIT

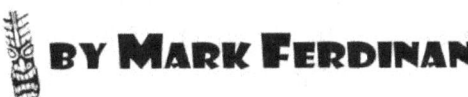 BY MARK FERDINAND

*EVERY TIKI HAS A SPIRIT*
By
Mark Ferdinand


Copyright © 2018 by Mark Ferdinand

markferdinandbooks@gmail.com

*Mark Ferdinand is the author of*
*Fortune on the Spectrum*
*You're Gonna' Get Bit!*
*and*
*The Autistic Prankster*

"Tikis are never finished, only abandoned"

*Greg Brady?*

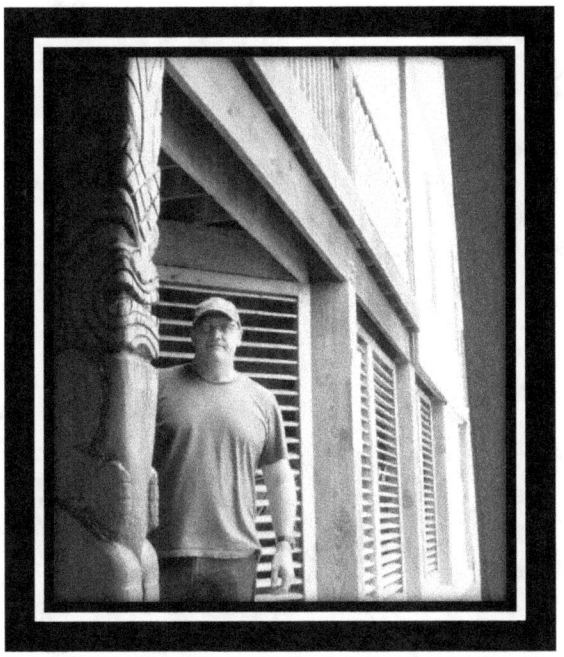

*Author standing by his work*

## The Quest Begins

I have always been a person with hobbies. Correction, I have always been a person with *too many* hobbies. Many interests have come and gone during the course of my life. I get fixated on some endeavor and want to know all about it. Often the interest fades or something new comes along.

It is somewhat surprising then that the hobby of carving tikis seems to have stuck with me for a while. Although I have always had a comfort with creative pursuits and art, most of my creations and attempts at different outlets were one-time projects. One activity that I had next to zero experience with was wood carving.

I believe that it was on my fifteenth birthday that my mother bought me a beginner's wood carving set. It was a quality set that had all the chisels to get a young man started in the hobby quite adequately. I lived in Colorado and made frequent visits to the forest so finding a piece of wood to carve was never a setback to getting started.

No, the problem was with my numerous other interests and distractions of being a young man. So the chisels would sit in their original box in pristine condition.

They sat in this box through my teenage years. They sat in my parents' home when I went to college. I then packed them into another box where they sat in Southern California where I lived for twelve years. They then sat in yet another box after a move to Padre Island off the Texas coast. This carving set went unused and unblemished for no less than twenty eight years.

I was in my back yard on an island which sits in a 9B growing zone. I was engaged in, yes, my latest hobby, tropical gardening. I had just planted a new palm tree and was admiring my developing garden. I was focused on tropical plants, trying to mimic the look and feel of Hawaii as best as the local climate would allow.

Here we cannot grow coconut trees, at least not for long. They are not quite tough enough to withstand the rare, but quite possible frost that may or may not come during winter. We can, however, enjoy many other palms and plants from tropical regions.

I began to think that the garden was missing something. Some type of ornament suitable for a tropical setting. This is when the thought occurred to me that a giant tiki carving, maybe one as tall as a person, would add a fantastic look to the yard when nestled among the palms, ti plants, and hibiscus flowers.

It was not many years earlier that I lived in Southern California. I recalled that the Home Depot there used to sell tiki carvings of a sort in the garden section. This should be easy then, I shall simply go to the local outlet here and pick one up!

As it turns out, inventory varies between locations, and offerings may come and go. No tikis were to be found there or anywhere else in my area. Were the hell was I going to find a five foot tiki for my yard?

It was at this time that I had a recollection of once owning a wood carver's set. Maybe I still had it somewhere, packed up in a box deep in the bowels of my garage.

If I could find this set, maybe I could take a stab at making a small tiki. Maybe it would look halfway decent. If something like that were to happen, maybe I could make a second attempt on a large log and set it in my yard. Later, if someone asked, I could brag that I made it myself. Maybe it would not look as nice as the work of a "professional" tiki carver, but not bad for a homemade attempt.

I told myself that if I could find the old box of chisels without having to tear the garage apart, then that would be the deciding factor in giving this a try. I believe it was the third drawer that I pulled and peeked into that revealed the carving set box in plain view. I removed the box lid and each chisel was there, unblemished, shiny, waiting.

## The First One - The Worst One

I'm not sure what would make a person feel that they had any sort of a talent, ability or any other offering after creating such a monstrosity. I, however, propped this piece up, gazed at it proudly, and proclaimed "I am onto something here!"

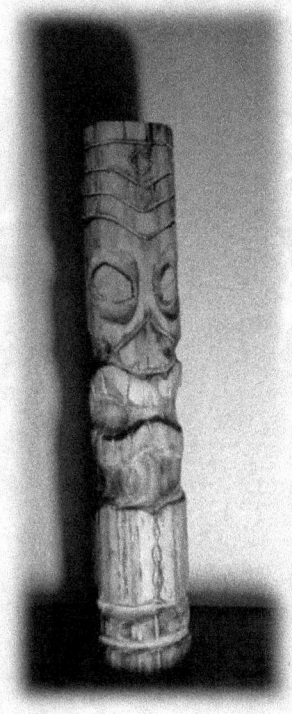

Maybe it was the pathetically sunken eyes, the two globs claiming to be fists, or the total disregard toward depth or detail. Maybe it was the look it had of a toothless ninety-year-old man. Possibly it was my fine stain job worthy of a master craftsman. Whatever it was that spoke to me, it must have said- *Some sucker would pay money for these.*

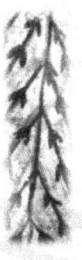

*In the days before us all, all of this land and all of this earth was covered with water. Water that was clear. Water that man could drink. All of this earth was not as you see, all of its contents nonexistent. Nothing on earth but water.*

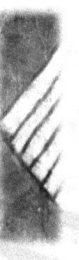

## Depth!

I realized what I neglected to provide in my first attempt. Holding back from gouging deeply into the wood will never yield any kind of interest or obvious resemblance to anything appealing to the human eye.

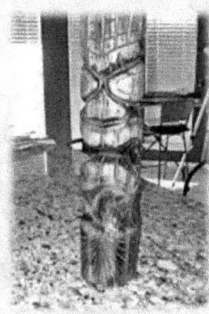

This is the next attempt after coming to this realization. A marked improvement, but still with a ridiculous looking mouth, with barely detectable lips. A nose devoid of detail. Fancy stain job though!

I ended up putting this guy on eBay, and it sold! Of course, as a novice eBay seller, I ended up paying way too much shipping out of pocket, causing me only to make a few dollars profit. A lesson learned but a boost to my ego that someone purchased a piece of art that I had made.

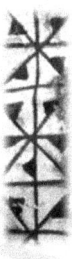

*The water began to recede, soon to almost vanish. As the water vanished it revealed grasses and plants that sought to fill the land. Some, over many, many moons became trees.*

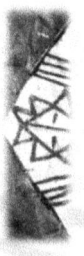

## Eyes of a New Style

Flirting with a remote resemblance to a tiki here. And - whoa now- there seems to be a tiny hint of a lip line! Someone is starting to realize that teeth don't just appear from out of the skin of the face. An attempt at an elaborate headress was made.

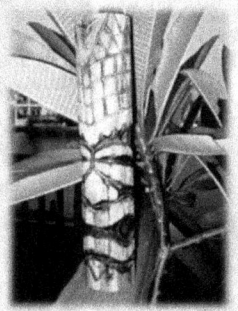

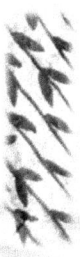

*Except for the vast salty ocean, the water would now be found only in lakes, ponds, rivers and streams. Rain came and kept the rivers and streams running, the lakes and ponds filled with more of this sweet water.*

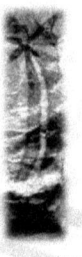

## Clunky Progress

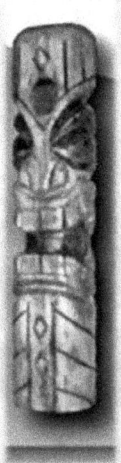

Upon the realization of how gums work, I sealed the deal on this one. Going bold, I stopped holding back and added depth to my cuts overall. I was able to come up with more realism to the nose and by sheer accident, created a bulbous new style of eye. A style since abandoned. Some unfounded confidence inspired me to dazzle the beast with diamond shapes and- *ooo lines!*

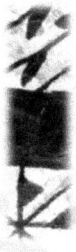

*There was no moving, living animal to be found upon the earth. There was only the hills, grasses, trees, lakes, rivers, ocean and sky.*

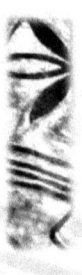

## Almost a Tiki

Celebrating the basics here. I believe I finally created an acceptable, identifiable and basic tiki. Nothing elaborate, but effective. Gave this to my parents for Christmas. *Awwww…*

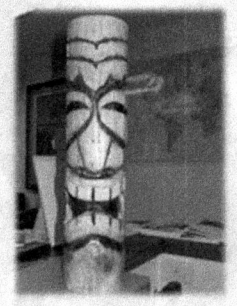

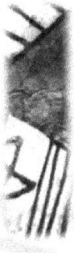

EVERY TIKI HAS A SPIRIT

One day there came from the ocean a great fish. It is not known how long he had lived, or why he had come to be. This was the great fish Falea'efe that had pulled himself to shore to see this new earth.

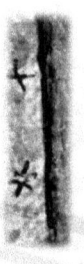

## Geometric and Soulless

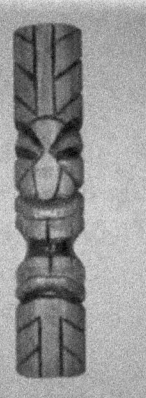

Perfecting bilateral symmetry in this one. Nothing technically wrong here besides the overly carved mouth cavity. Very geometric and angular which, for a tiki, makes it somewhat soulless. Appealing, but with low spirit level. With a flat back, can be either hung on a wall or set on a shelf.

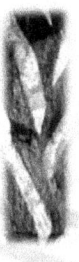

In the sky there was only the moon and on the earth there was only Falea'efe. As the moon made its journey through the sky, one day it looked down to find him, Falea'efe looked up, and the two at last met.

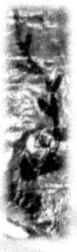

### The First Giant

Having created six mediocre tikis, I must have felt that I was ready for the big time. *Big*, meaning a five-foot tiki. The entire reason I began carving tikis in the first place, was to

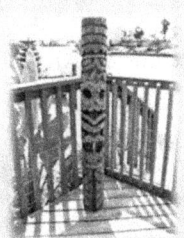 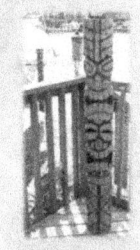

have a jumbo tiki in my yard. Something I still do not have. Not ready for any kind of attempt at a body, instead I created a double-sided, two-headed tiki. A mirror image of both faces front and back. Surprisingly ambitious and not a failure, with the exception of the poor stain job.

This tiki and all four of his warrior heads now resides outside of his natural tropical habitat, but has a fresh new stain

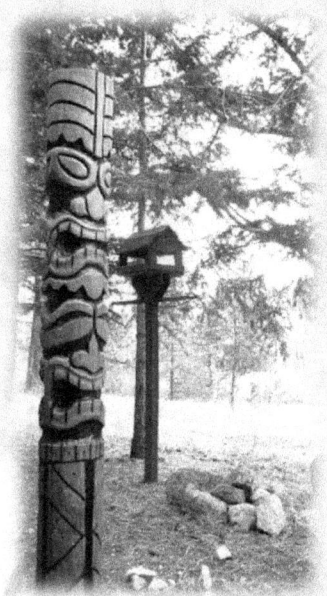

job. He lives at ten thousand feet in the Rocky Mountains, guarding a cabin from bear attacks.

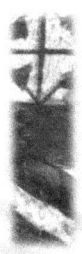

The moon and Falea'efe had many discussions. The moon told stories of the sky, after which Falea'efe told his stories of the earth. Each did this in exchange until their stories ran out.

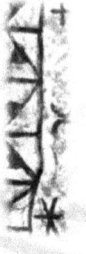

A word here about using fire as a "staining" tool. It is a very appealing idea when you are talking about creating primitive art. Nothing more primitive than fire! I attempted this technique on several of my first tikis with the use of a

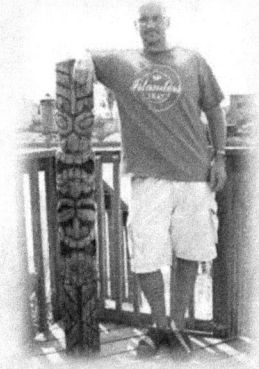

blow torch and even a tiki torch. I had seen it done by others. Having looked at both mine and theirs, I came to the conclusion that it looks like hell.

There may be others that use this technique with success and like it, but I have abandoned it gladly and my tikis have since turned out for the better.

My parents came from out of state for a Thanksgiving visit. Being my biggest supporters and encouragers for my artistic attempts, they paid way too much for this piece and permanently displayed it in their yard. I now had no choice but to continue this pursuit.

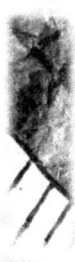

"I have an idea" said Falea'efe. "Perhaps a man and a woman should be created. Created so that all the oceans, all the lakes, all the rivers, all the grasses, all the trees, and all the hills of the earth can be enjoyed. Perhaps then, more stories shall be created.

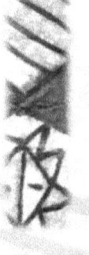

## Word of Your Work has Spread

Even selling to family can get some chatter going. Having seen my work during the same Thanksgiving visit, my brother showed photos to a friend, who decided he needed a 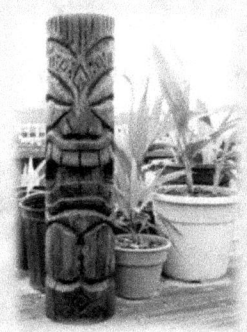 tiki. I had since began working on a couple more pieces and had a few for him to choose from. The friend chose this sturdy, medium piece in dark stain.

This was my first serious venture into adding other parts of the body besides faces. My first attempt at touching fists with what I will call moderate success. Also solidifying my pursuit of optimal depth. Sale made to my second stranger!

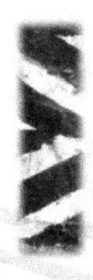

"A perfectly fine idea!" replied the moon. "I shall be the one to make them. For I am of the sky and eternal. They shall have my light and shall last eternally."

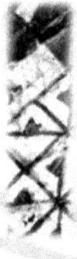

## I Brought You a Piece of Wood

As I took notice of outside appreciation for my work, it occurred to me that my sister had a wedding coming up. Instead of racking my brain to find a unique gift, I decided to 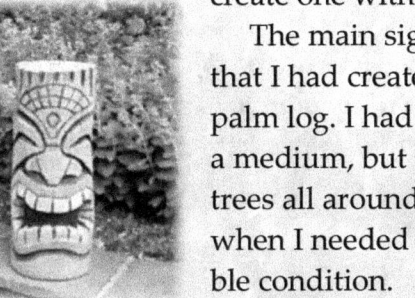 create one with my own little hands.

The main significance of this piece is that I had created my first work from a palm log. I had been dying to try palm as a medium, but though I lived with palm trees all around me, no logs were around when I needed them, or were not in suitable condition.

I finally stumbled upon the perfect palm log on the side of a road one day. After shaving off the outer layer of bark, I went to work. Palm is a wonderful medium for tiki work, yet has its limits in practicality for some applications. For an indoor decorative tiki the palm log in good condition is perfect. The end product was barkless and smooth. A unique material to work with indeed.

I was actually a tad nervous about how it would be received, but it seemed to be a hit at the reception.

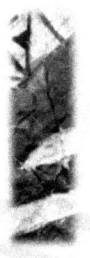

Falea'efe responded. "True, you are of the sky and eternal, but I am of the earth. Man and woman are to be part of the earth, they should be created by that which is familiar and at home with the earth. You know only the way of the sky."

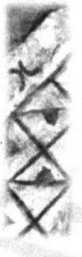

## Commissioned Art

My brother made a request for a medium sized tiki after my parents and sister got theirs. Not above utilizing family 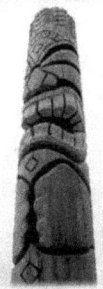 as a customer base, I agreed to create one for him for a modest fee. Listen folks, this was a fledgling business at best at the time and I needed the money, so of course I charged him for two months of my spare time!

Going back to hard, treated pine. This carving made me proud to the point that I wished it was part of my patio décor. I polished my skills at creating clenched fists that are recognizable as such, and the mouth was wide, deep and grand.

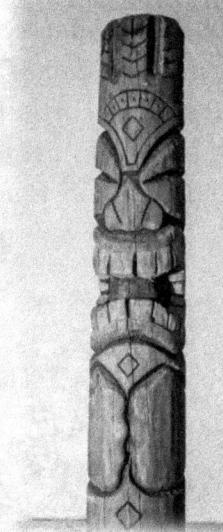

*Photo by Michael Hockmuller*

Two feet tall and menacing. I was starting to get a feel for what my version of a tiki should be.

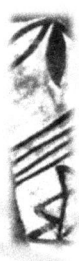

"Yes" the moon replied. "While true that you are of the earth on which man and woman will walk, like you they shall grow tired one day of walking and die they will. This like all things of the earth. I know Falea'efe, for I see and watch all of the earth. Let it be I that create them, that give them my light and save them from this tiring.

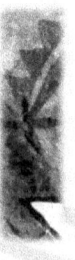

## Deep Ebony

Having the hankering for the creation of another jumbo tiki, I got ahold of another ten-foot treated log and cut it in

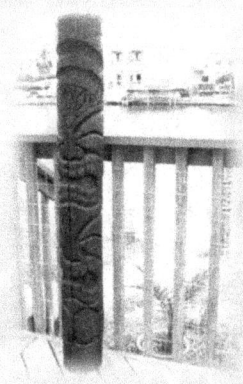

half. This time I had a vision of creating an all-black tiki. I had seen smaller ones in photographs and liked the look. I imagined that a jumbo black tiki would be very imposing and dramatic.

I spent extra time on this tiki, taking care to make my cuts deep and distinct so that they would not be diminished under a black stain.

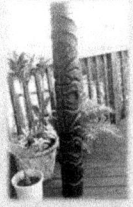

Upon completion I was pretty pleased with myself. *This one is bound to sell fast,* I thought. Nope.

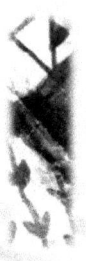

"But if you, moon, create them, they will know nothing of the changing earth" countered Falea'efe. "They will know only the distant, unchanging way of the sky. They will live eternally, but be in life only minimally and only remotely. No, it shall be I that create them, and as I am closest to earth it shall be thus."

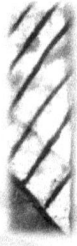

## Why Do This?

The low point of my tiki creating days followed what I thought was a high point with previous orders. No more requests were forthcoming. I had built up a small inventory

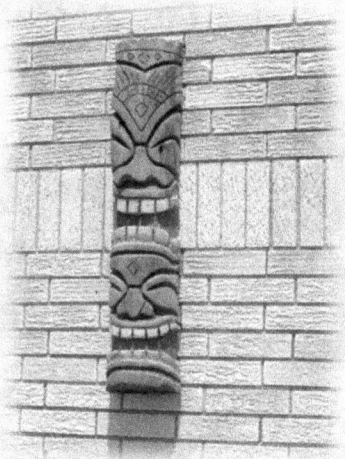

and submitted online ads to both eBay and Craigslist, I even built a web site. Interest was flat, truthfully it was nonexistent.

I continued with my work however, at least for a while. I found a large palm log on the beach that had a flat back. If I could tikify this log it may look nice hanging from a wall!

I finished it up over the next couple of weeks. No buyers were interested in any of my other work, but I liked this one and hung it on my outside wall over the patio.

Months went by and I had moved on. I pretty much stopped tiki carving due to lack of sales. I figured it was a fun little phase, not unlike others I had gone through. I was happy with what I had learned, and figured that one day, if I felt like it, I would go back to my original plan and make a big tiki for my yard, and that would be that. Then I got an email.

Living on an island, I felt that surely there was a market for people that wanted to decorate their bars, yards or pools with a tiki carving. Where were they? Well, one finally found me.

I met my first local customer that was a genuine tiki fan. He had found my web site and wanted to have a look at some of my carvings. He came over and we had a great visit discussing tikis, and he was impressed with my work.

He liked my work so much that he was ready to make a purchase. He ended up buying the flat-backed palm wall tiki. I was so grateful that I offered to re-stain it for him, as it had been baking in the sun for a while.

I told him that I was not making tikis anymore and he was appalled. He insisted that I continue and that interest would eventually come. What could I do but listen to the man?

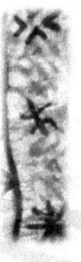

"No fish!" The angered moon warned. "It shall not be you, it shall be I!" "No rock!" Falea'efe defied. "It shall be I!"

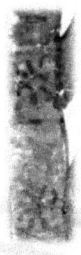

## Taking Another Look

Getting back to carving, I decided to pay more attention to various existing styles, the popular, traditional and geographical. I purchased a tiki on a Maui visit many years ago, and was told that the carver was Tongan. From then on I believed there to be a traditional "Tongan" tiki style, only to

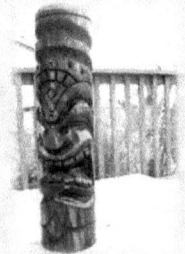

find out that it was most likely a personal style of a tiki carver who happened to be Tongan. Clear as mud?

Either way I began an appreciation for "Tongan" tikis and made an attempt at one here. Living in coastal Texas, I had access only to inferior wood to that of the Tongan,

but feel that it was a fair representation with what I had to work with, and my own interpretation added as well.

I will say that there is something very difficult about mimicking this style. It is hard to put my finger on it even to this day. There is something about the eye position, nose and upper lip that proves elusive to duplicate, yet I seem to find a way.

Word of mouth from a former co-worker brought this piece to another new customer!

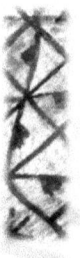

The two exchanged angrily back and forth in this way and for eons of time. They did this until they tired and could no longer continue. Falea'efe returned to the ocean, the moon moved on to other skies.

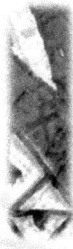

## Tiki with a Body

Of course a new customer is awesome, but what's better than a *repeat* customer? The island fan that encouraged me to continue carving asked me to create a new medium-sized

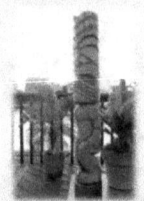

piece for him. This would be my first tiki with a full body, which I was awfully nervous about attempting.

It was a long and tedious learning experience to carve out a full body. I took my time and felt that I came up with a convincing finished product. This was also the first tiki, and one of the few I have made, without teeth. Many people are not fans of a toothless tiki, but I think that they should reconsider this stance.

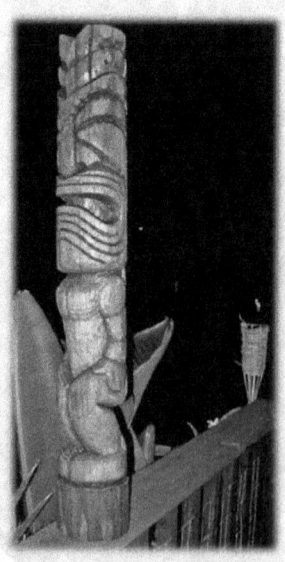

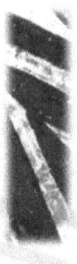

Each stewed in anger, even as they recognized the truth in what the other was saying. Each spent time in ponderance over what next to do.

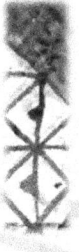

## Kinda' Tonga

One of the smaller pieces I had turned my attention to. Smaller tikis are a nice change of pace from the jumbo size, as they can be worked on while relaxing in a chair, as op-

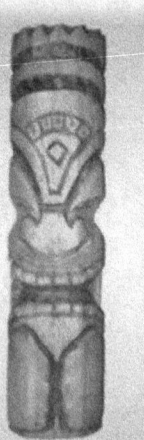

posed to wrestling a huge log.

Here I combined the Tongan/Maui style with the double fists I had an on-going fascination with. I also added my own style of crest to the head-dress.

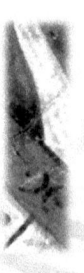

While Falea'efe was closest to the earth and could create man and woman all his own, he knew that his creation would not be what it could without the moon. While the moon knew that he could strike down Falea'efe for creating man and woman without him, he knew that they could not thrive as beings of the earth without him.

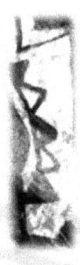

## Tattooed Tiki

Making another small, flat-backed tiki. I feel that I caught a good rhythm here. This tiki began my venture into the addition of tattoos to some of my work. The more I learned

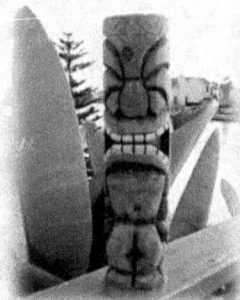

about traditional Polynesian tattoos, the more I felt that they would be a nice enhancement to my tikis. I don't use them on all my pieces, but I love having this option.

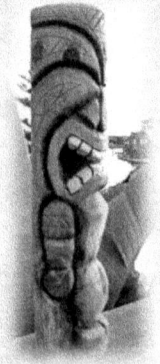

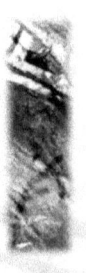

The moon inched toward the beach after much time had passed. Falea'efe saw the light at the ocean's surface and crawled from the beach once again. The two finally met at the same spot as before, now humble in tone.

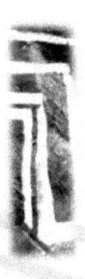

## Four-Foot Palm with Full Body

After acquiring a new palm log, I was delighted to try out a full body tiki in this medium. The soft wood shaved away with ease compared to the hard treated pine I am so used to dealing with.

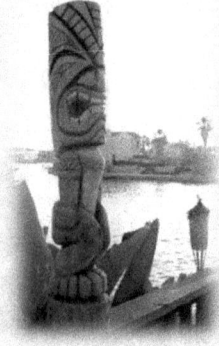

There is plenty that I would do over again on this piece, but his short little arms would be at the top of the list if I had the chance for only one thing to correct. Same goes for the elephant legs. More dabbling in tattoo work here.

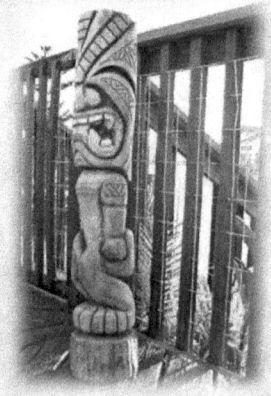

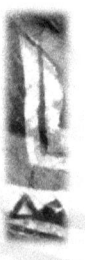

The moon spoke first. "As you have put forth such a noble idea, please allow me to put forth now one as well." Falea'efe bowed his head in reverence. "To be sure great moon." The moon continued. "We must tread forward in such a creation with thoughts that are best for what we create, not that which is best for ourselves."

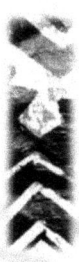

## Enter the Art Walk

I was hearing more and more about a local art walk held annually in my area. By the time I had considered participating, it was only a few weeks away. I had only a few completed tikis in my inventory, so I needed to get a few more done and done quickly, or I would have to wait another year to take part.

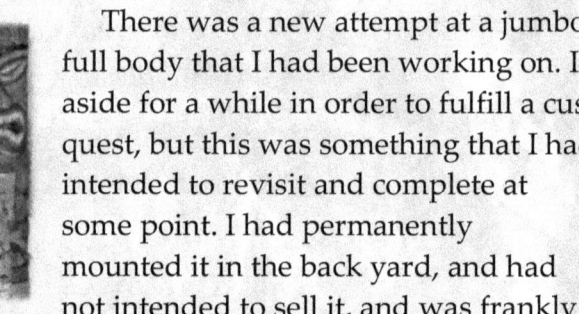

There was a new attempt at a jumbo tiki with a full body that I had been working on. I had put it aside for a while in order to fulfill a custom tiki request, but this was something that I had intended to revisit and complete at some point. I had permanently mounted it in the back yard, and had not intended to sell it, and was frankly not at all pleased with how it was coming along. I felt that it would be good enough as a yard piece, which was the reason I wanted to make tikis to begin with!

In desperation I uninstalled it from the mount and took a second look at it as a potential art walk piece. I did some more shaping on the body, and improved the eyes that I felt I had messed up so badly. I added a new layer of stain and it started to look acceptable to sell at the show after all. Nothing great, but a step up from what it was.

"You speak sense Moon" Falea'efe agreed "and if I may add, such a being to enjoy this earth should be endowed not just with earthly attributes, but with those of the moon. Your soothing light is needed."

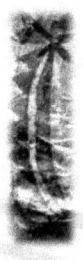

## Stump Salvage

As I was making my preparations for the show, I received an email from my local collector on the island about a palm stump sighting. I busted out the truck and found a nice, chunky palm stump just where he said it would be. I tossed it in the bed and brought it home.

This was my first experience in dealing with major imperfections in a palm log. There was a bit of rot in portions of this stump. I was, however, able to work around these imperfections or integrate them into the design.

My concern here was in selling a piece that may end up disintegrating on the customer at a later time.

Palm can be a remarkably resilient material it turns out. Years later I bumped into the man I sold it to and spoke to him about my concerns. He said that he experienced no issues of continued rot. These results vary of course with severity and location of the rot, and the environment in which the tiki is kept. But all turned out well after dry air won out over the moisture within.

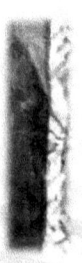

The moon offered, "Allow me to contribute just subtly. My light will not be seen when looking upon this man or woman, nor upon their own creations. My eternal light will be planted within them, to be summoned from within them, to be taken with them wherever they may go. I shall remain looking upon them from the sky, reflecting this light in different ways and at different times. Their earthly attributes I leave to you."

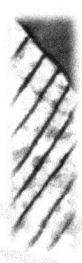

## Peddling my Wares

I ended up slapping together a display table for my pieces at the art walk. It was nice to see people stop and show interest at my table and ask questions about things that I had created.

It was an interesting feeling to sit at this event. I was taken back to my childhood when I ran my first lemonade stand. This was remarkably similar, but with many more potential customers showing obvious curiosity toward my work.

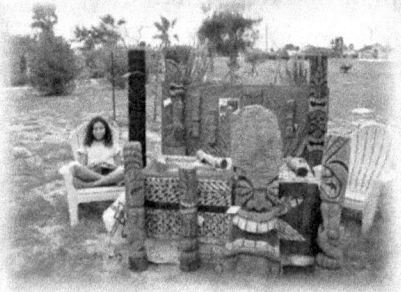

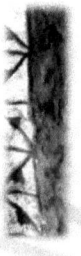

   *"You humble me with this task and with your generosity great moon." said Falea'efe "Today we shall create man and woman, I shall prepare them for this life on earth and you shall finish them with your light that lasts within them for their time on earth, and for eternity."*

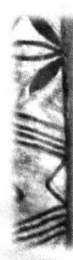

Of course they were mostly looky-loos. People from all walks of life and all ages were there, it should be no surprise that many had no idea what a tiki was. Most glanced and kept moving. I heard many a comment of "Ooo totem poles! How neat!" and off they went on their merry way.

Nevertheless, this was a great way to spend a Sunday with beautiful fall weather. My tikis were getting more exposure than I had ever experienced up to this point. We thoroughly enjoyed the day.

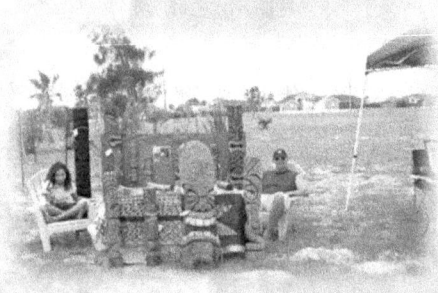

What I really enjoyed were the sales! The odd thing was that the two pieces that I had the least confidence in, were the ones that sold. I also sold a couple of the little guys in my inventory.

I was somewhat over the moon when I came home and counted my cash.

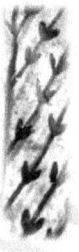

*The two worked together in fashioning man and woman. Falea'efe with the earthly qualities necessary to negotiate the habitat of the earth, and the moon to add his shine within them and the desire to look to the sky. They then worked together to add a new trait from their efforts and ponderings, that of discernment.*

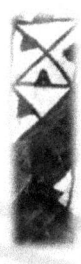

## Networking

With a tiki sitting at the home of each family member, I could only hope that here and there, more people from outside the family would take notice and interest. This occurred after a bit of time.

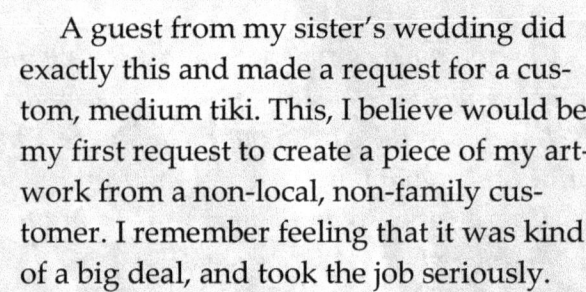

A guest from my sister's wedding did exactly this and made a request for a custom, medium tiki. This, I believe would be my first request to create a piece of my artwork from a non-local, non-family customer. I remember feeling that it was kind of a big deal, and took the job seriously.

The customer only specified size and allowed me freedom of design. She gave me a very reasonable amount of time to work and I sent her regular photo updates via email.

Having a flexible timeline also helped with my margins on shipping. Upon completion, using standard ground shipping was a much more inexpensive proposition than my eBay fiasco. The cost was very reasonable, and it arrived on time.

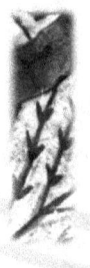

*The faculty of discernment would be used by man and woman to explore their world. To compare what they see, hear, and smell and match it to their desires.*

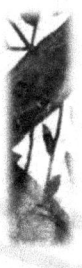

### New Boost of Interest

A few sales at the art show and a custom tiki request reinvigorated my efforts in tiki carving. I also made a few more people aware of my existence on the island, which put more eyes out on the alert for palm logs.

Helpful folks began to contact me when a good pile of logs were sighted in the area. This occurs once in a while when trees are being cut down and removed from resident homes for whatever reason. The logs are placed in brush piles and they wait for the city service to pick them up. If I get the word in time, I can make a few of them mine.

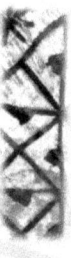

Man and woman were sent on their way on the earth, and Falea'efe and the moon looked upon them with pride. Man and woman moved through all that had been created, they even had children who had the light within given to them by the moon, yet still they appeared lost.

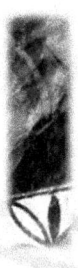

## Great, I'll Take Two

Between helpful fans and an inland windstorm near work, I was able to acquire both some new palm logs and a nice length of ash from a fallen tree. I created a front-bodied four-footer with a new style of leg positioning that I had never tried. I created a little guy from the ash log that ended

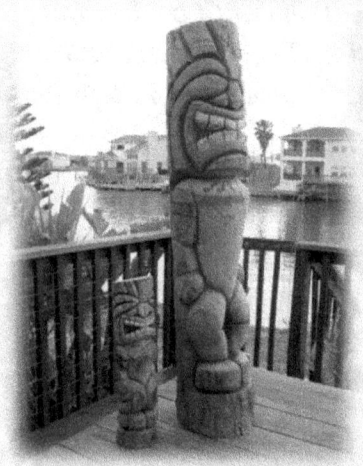

up looking like it was related to the bigger palm tiki. I called them Poppa and Boy.

I ended up selling both to a new customer that discovered me online. The perfect tiki customer actually. A gentleman with both a pool and a tiki bar. The big guy would stand guard over the pool, his little boy would greet the partygoers.

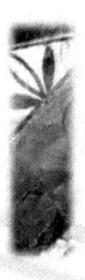

Falea'efe and the moon decided that their project was not complete. That man and woman would need pursuits, cravings, conflicts, staples, rewards, struggles, and triumphs in order to have meaning in their time on earth. Falea'efe and the moon began to add forces of deity to their world, this to give lesson to man, woman and all that they may create.

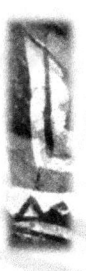

## Among My Favorites

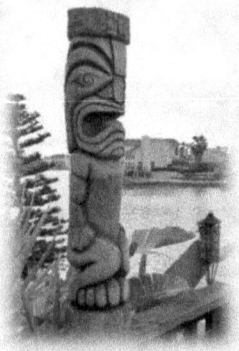

To this day, although my carvings have improved greatly since, this is still among my top favorite creations. The palm log had an existing unique shape that helped make it all come together.

I normally give teeth to my tikis, but some-

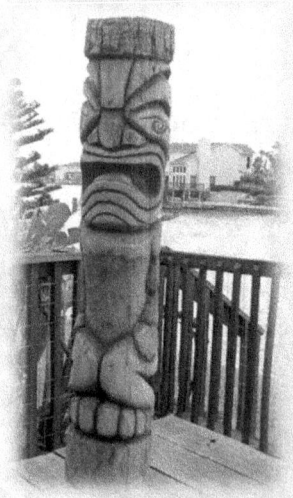

times a toothless tiki just works. It can give its own distinct look taken from its own unknown island. I continued my experimentation with adding tattoos.

In addition I included a modest tongue that is not quite being stuck out, but perhaps about to be, perhaps before per-

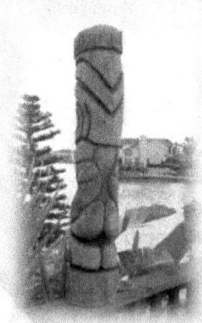

forming a haka. This remains my only tiki that sports a top knot, not unlike those of his Easter Island Moai cousins. I shall have to incorporate this idea again. Sometimes it all just comes together.

*The butt shot!*

*The god Niu was created. Niu was the god of survival. He took his place on the earth in the form of coconuts of infinite number. Through Niu, man and woman would always have remedy for thirst and hunger in elementary form. Niu would provide other uses as well in enhancing other foods and in use of its strong shell for tools, building and adornments.*

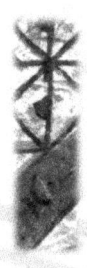

### Two Little Fellas

Coming back to the world of little tikis. Some customers want to get in on the tiki vibe but are not ready to go big. I need to expand these smaller offerings, even though my ideal vision of tikis has always been that they be made enormous.

I neglect these little guys at my own peril. Why not expand the amount of people that possess my work rather than 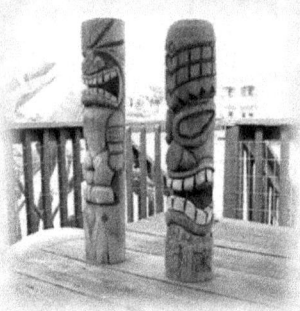 focus on the few that acquire the big fellas? There is what pulls me, and then there is what makes sense. Turtles, hibiscus, and tattoos carved into these bread and butter tikis.

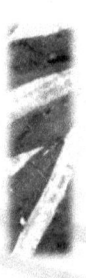

Next the goddess Talo was created. She had her spirit both above ground in leaf and below ground in root. Talo too fills the hunger of man and woman, but is more demanding of effort than that of Niu. With patience and time though, she is abundant. Niu compliments her.

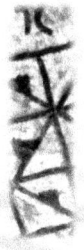

## Canyon Brown Palm Beefcake

Then between the jumbo and the shelf size, there are the mediums. The step up from the beginner tiki if you will. This seems to end up being the ideal gift size for a lot of people.

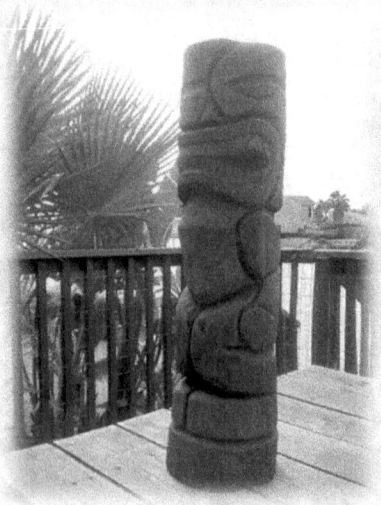

Nothing that is going to be a burden, either size wise in the home, or in the pocketbook. More impressive as a gift than the little knickknack tikis, as it makes a statement in the room.

This was a solid medium palm piece stained with dark brown deck stain and ebony stained eyes.

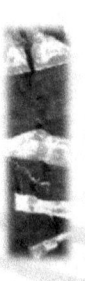

*Heimoa was created as the bird god. Birds of the sky and those that only walk the earth near the homes of man and woman. Heimoa provides the meat and eggs of birds to nourish man and woman beyond Nui and Talo. Heimoa takes many forms and provides feathers of all size and color for adornments.*

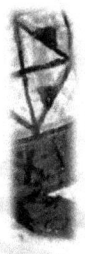

## Crested Chiefs and Fists of Fury

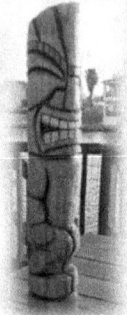

While I fretted over the strategies of tiki sales, some customers mercifully made the decisions for me. The sister's wedding guest had already caught on to the concept of the ideal medium tiki gift. She ordered another one for yet another friend. Boy if I could just have ten gift-minded ladies like this a month to cater to I could do this gig for a living!

Around this same time I was contacted by the son of a local islander. Seems the father was a real tikiphile that I hadn't met yet. The son requested a custom five-footer with Airborne jump patches tattooed on the chest, a first for me, but why not? Two tribal shoulder tattoos were added for fun.

Upon delivery of the completed five-footer the son decided to throw in another gift for old dad.

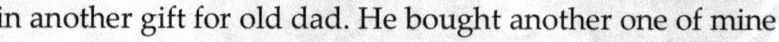

He bought another one of mine that had gone unsold for quite some time since its creation. This was a unique tiki that I had taken a liking too. On a whim this carving focused on giant fists pounding together, which I think created a *striking* effect in proportion to the rest of his body.

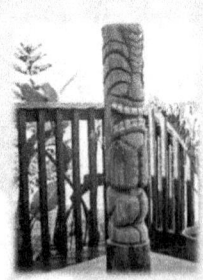

## The Eve of Tiki

Taking a dive into the unknown. I had thought about making a female tiki, just to do it. I put it off for quite some time due to lack of inspiration. Then I had a look at one of the logs I had acquired, I stared at it for a while. The log had curves, curves in all the right places.

The natural bark of the log would serve as her hula skirt. I think I failed miserably with her poor face and breasts, but then again, how realistic are my male tikis? At this point all I wanted was for her to be recognizable as a female, not as model material. Could anyone ever love her?

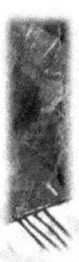

The god Sahonu was created as the god of the ocean turtle. With effort the meat of the turtle could be had for variety on its own or with the plants and Talo provided for all. Sahonu also gives the spirit of defense. A great shell can be used to shield, to protect the head or to carry that which is valued.

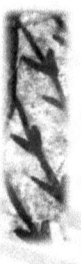

## Round Two in the Park

Another year had come and gone and I was now prepared for the next island art walk. I had amassed a nice selection of small, medium and large tikis to offer the passing looky loos. One standout was my tallest tiki yet. A six-footer!

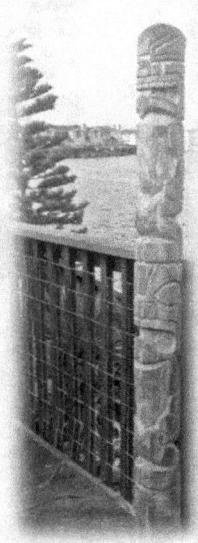

Not only was he tall, there were two of him. A strong, toothless, warrior standing on a pedestal. He supported another imposing guard, this one with my first implementation of a menacing tongue. Both chaps sported Marquesan-inspired eyes and everything combined to exude intimidation.

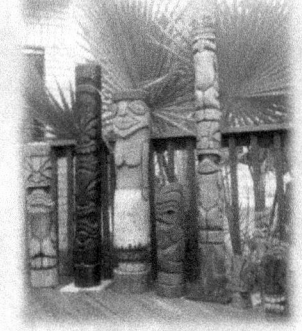

Some things just come together and some things just sell themselves. This six-footer attracted attention. People loved it but it was a bit pricy for most. I didn't need most to like it, I just needed the perfect set of eyes to see it.

Enter the perfect set of eyes. A chap with a certain amount of success under his belt and with an aging tiki fan for a father happened by. It also happened to be that his father was having a birthday soon.

With only limited haggling, I had a wad of bills in my hand and the man carried his carved log off to his vehicle, both of us smiling all the way.

*Puavao was created as the greatest god of all nourishment and that of the wild boar. Puavao is the spirit of the great prize, festival, and challenge. Hunting the hills seeks the spirit of Puavao in both the effort and the rewards of success. Summoned for training and battle.*

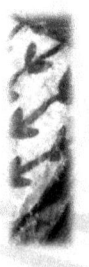

## You Can Just Walk

Now what can be said when my tikis take on such power that it causes a mother to sacrifice the comfort of her own

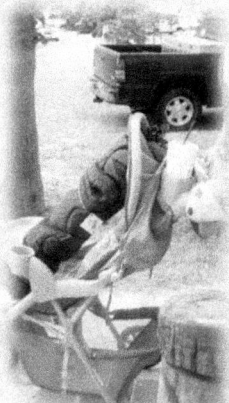

child in order to haul away her tiki purchase in the child's stroller? I learned that day that I must be careful of the hidden magic emitting from within these creations.

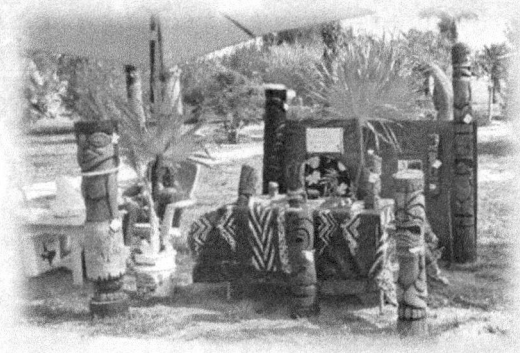

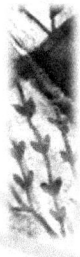

The moon interjected in the creation of all things that man and woman may thrive upon on the earth. It occurred to him that he should pay tribute to Falea'efe. "In ponderance of your noble idea to create and provide for man and woman, I propose that you be honored Falea'efe. Let Falea'efe be the god of all fish of the ocean, lakes and rivers."

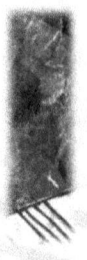

## Adorned with Jewels of the Sea

Something a bit different that I tried after the art walk season. Also something that has yet to be embraced by a customer or myself. Perhaps because I veered from the formula

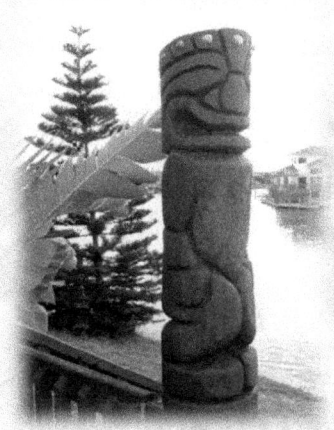

and added a smile, something that a true tiki does not do. This combined with the lack of teeth could make a carving that is no longer tiki. I was excited about the embedded crown of shells, something that I had not seen done before, but so far I am his lone fan. So I suppose he'll be tagging along with me for a while.

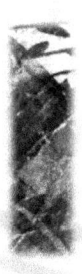

"Let they be sought by man and woman when desired, that they may be discovered in all sizes, shapes and colors and looked upon in wonder. May they be found in numbers that match the stars of my great skies."

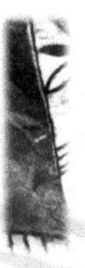

## Stumpy but Wind Proof

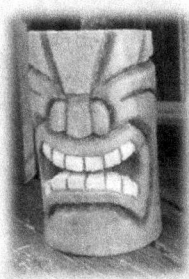

Besides the seashell king, this was a tremendous lull of a year for tiki work. A busy life took over, maybe a lack of inspiration, maybe a shortage of good logs. I did, toward the end of the year, strike some luck in the log department though.

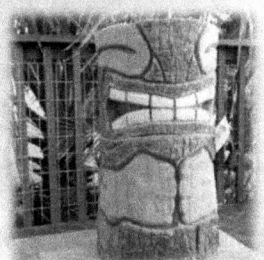

I put out two chunky, solid heads that were basic but appealing.

They were meant to be sold at the upcoming art show, as we will see in the next photo, but were snapped up from Craigslist a day before. A sweet couple from the next town over travelled enthusiastically to pick them up and grace them beside their pool.

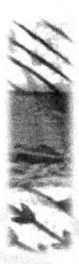

*Uti came to earth as the goddess of dance, cooking, shelter and protection. She takes the form of leaves of all colors, sizes and shapes. Her bounty serves in the wrapped cooking of rewards of Niu, Talo, Sahonu, Heimoa, Sahonu, Puavao, and the fish of Falea'efe. She adorns and protects man and woman from rain and sun, and decorates them in dance. Her materials help create wares of the home and protection of its walls.*

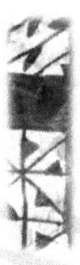

## Seven Offerings

Minus the two sales just before the show, this ended up being my seven offerings for the art walk this time around. As seen here, the beautiful black five-footer still with no takers. The female stays again as well. This was a tight year for folks, and in tight years the little tikis make the few sales. So this year's show sold only a couple of little guys, and was mostly just a pleasant day in the sun.

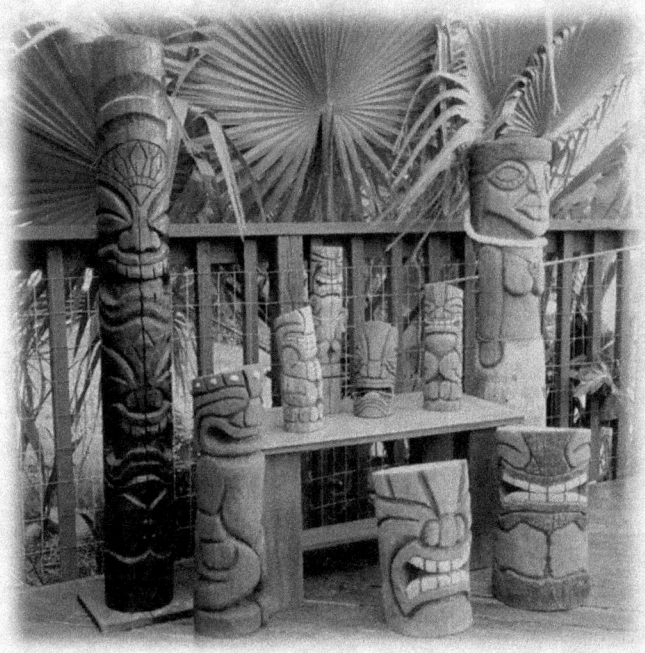

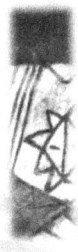

*Mahupele became the goddess of fire, sun and wind. Found from the great fire rivers and the great fire mountain from which they flow, man and woman may take fire back home with them. Mahupele gives a good man the power to create fire by his own efforts as well. Her winds control fire and allows travel of all things of the earth that make use of her.*

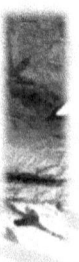

## Time to Up My Game

I came to the unpleasant realization that I was beginning to stagnate in my artistic progress. I was putting out product but putting a self-imposed limit on my capabilities. For this next

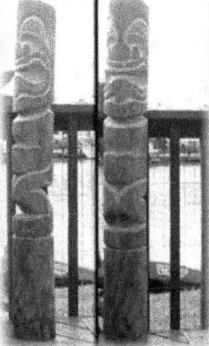

five-footer, I would take my time, pursue a piece that was high in detail and complexity, and attempt new techniques. Here are photos of pre-completion and pre-staining of something that I became quite proud of.

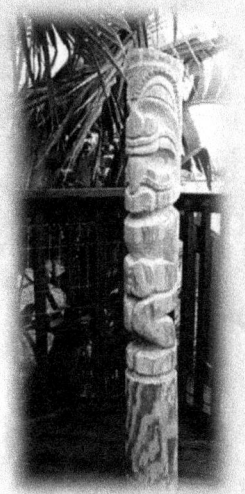

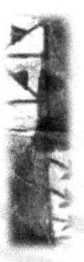

*Tohumoko is the god of artists. Tohumoko overtakes certain men which present carvings of wood, stone and bone. Designs on the skin of man and woman come from those with the spirit of Tohumoko.*

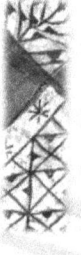

## The New Approach

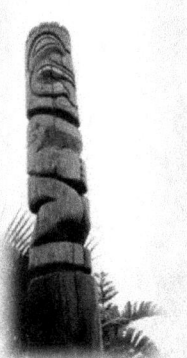

As said, I had decided that I should reach for a higher level in some of my work. This finished five-footer expressed that. While I would still crank out some basic tikis in order to have a volume of work, I learned that I should always strive to create high end pieces as well.

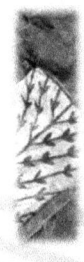

I think I achieved that here with the complexities attempted. The attention-getting tongue, the lifelike fists, and the detailed facial tattoos all contributed to this goal.

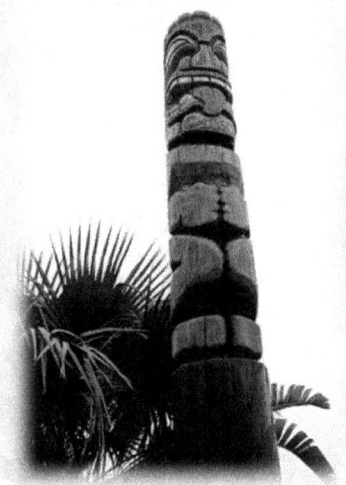

Those that create canoes of war and fishing, those that create the fishing nets, those that explore the sea and take its fish and animals, all succeed or fail at the hands of Katangaroa. Katangaroa is the god of all seafaring and creators of related ocean tools. He often takes the form of a whale or a wave, but can be found in the lakes and rivers of the earth as well.

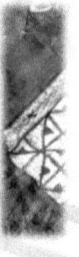

## One of my Few Freebies

This palm stump was tikified in order to show my appreciation for a long time customer and supporter of my work. He always looks out for cut palm logs on the curbs of island residents and shoots me an alert when he finds them. This log was among a big batch that he discovered.

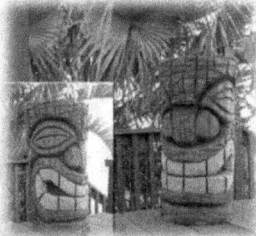

Straying again from my no-smiles rule a bit, but I think it worked out here. I integrated the bark of the palm into this design, something I like to do when the bark is interesting and in particularly good condition as it was in this case.

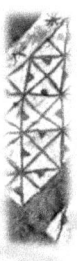

Foatalo was created as the god of rain, clouds and mist. Foatalo, along with Mahupele and Katangaroa could work together to create storms of the ocean and of the earth. She mostly works on her own to provide all the fresh water of the earth and feeding of its lakes and rivers. Offerings are made at the top of the highest of mountains to appease and to thank her.

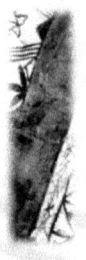

## Ahhh, Freshly Sanded

Sometimes I don't look forward to staining over freshly sanded wood that can look so beautiful. I realize that the look can't last, so at least I can enjoy it in photos when I remember to take them. Here are three stacked tiki heads completed from the batch of logs mentioned.

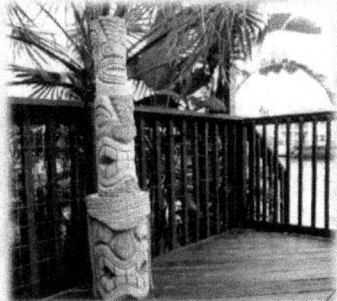

Up top I have some dabbling into the style of the Marquesas Island tikis. In the middle, an integrated bark nose. Holding them up is a nice chunky palm stump of a basic design with some exposed bark as a helmet.

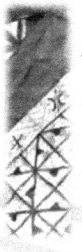

Peah'rapa is the god of stone, tools and jewels. The spirit of Peah'rapa is found in the construction of walls and the work of specialized tradesman. Pearls of the sea and jewels of the earth are the rare representations of his greatest gift of luck and fortune.

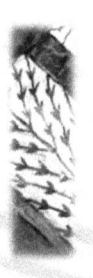

## Heard You Missed Me

My offerings for the annual art walk this time around. The black five-footer was still with me, as was the warrior hula queen. After lackluster sales the previous year, I was hoping for some better results this time around.

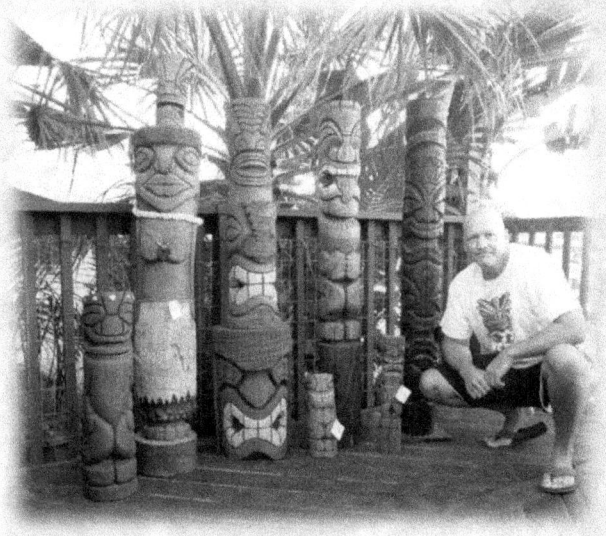

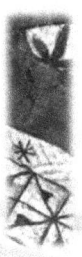

The moon and Falea'efe found man and woman still to be lost in their world. They were much like the other animals of the earth in their life from day to day. A life of seeking food and surviving was found to be incomplete.

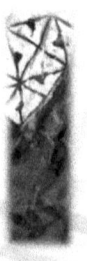

### Now We're Talkin'

Better results happened indeed! My detailed five-footer attracted a lot of interest and illustrated that the extra attention to detail could pay off. It didn't take long before it caught the eye of just the right viewer with just the right wallet. It can be seen here on its way to its new home.

I considered the day to be a success already, but there was much more to come. I finally unloaded the black five-footer!

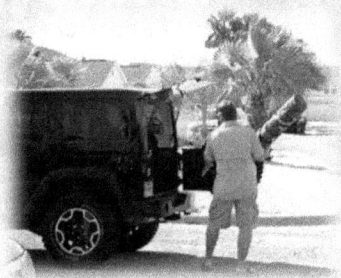

Neither I, nor the customer could understand what took so long for it to sell. All three of the new stacked tiki heads sold as well, along with one of the little guys. This was surely an art walk to remember.

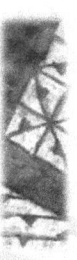

"We must give man and woman the gift of feeling" said the Moon, "On this we agree" Falea'efe added. "We have given them much, but the infinite colors of the earth, the ocean, the animals and the flowers seem not to affect them." The moon and Falea'efe agreed that a number of new spirits should be available to man and woman.

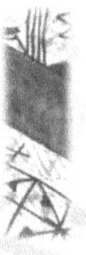

## Get in Sweetie

Maybe I got cocky, maybe I got busy, but the next year produced very little in the way of tiki work. I showed up to the art walk the following year with only five pieces to offer and

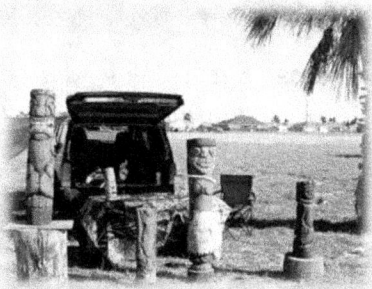

sold only two. One was a little guy, the other was the queen that had been a wallflower for so long! A woman saw in her, everything that I loved, and she bought her to grace the deck of her pool.

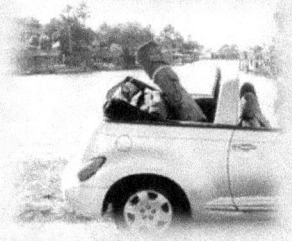

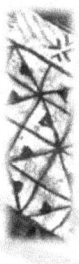

Hau'ia is the goddess of happiness. She is that which touches the spirit of man and woman at joyful moments of festivity, childbirth, and fortune. Hau'ia graces man and woman when they are at their most dutiful toward each other and toward others.

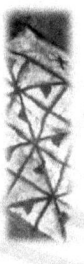

## An Oddball Email

Checking on one of my old email addresses, I noticed a message that, for a change, did not appear to be spam. It was an inquiry about having some tikis created. Specifically, it was requesting a quote to have around ten, eight-foot tikis created.

Now let me say that I have had inquiries before. What usually happens is that someone gets a wild idea that they would like to have some tikis made for their back yard project. They ask how much something like that would cost, I give them a fair estimate, and they quickly move on from the idea. This is tedious and time-consuming work, I tend to charge much less than what most carvers would for it.

I replied with an estimate to what such a large amount of tikis created in what I thought would be a reasonable time frame would cost. What happened was just what I expected, I heard nothing back from them.

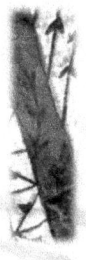

The god Kauhaatu is he who overcomes the spirit with sorrow. Upon a tragic death or moments of misfortune, Kauhaatu visits until he deems the proper time has passed. His role does not please him but is one that gives man and woman their place of prominence on the earth over fish, bird and animals of the land.

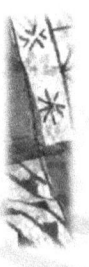

## More Female Action

The sale of my first tiki temptress gave me another boost of momentum. *The world needs more female tikis-* I decided. I got straight to work on another palm log that I could see a rough womanly shape within. I found that creating a tiki with a complimentary female appearance was no easy task. Male tikis are supposed to be ugly and menacing. My view is that the female version should possess exaggerated features but be distinctly feminine at the same time.

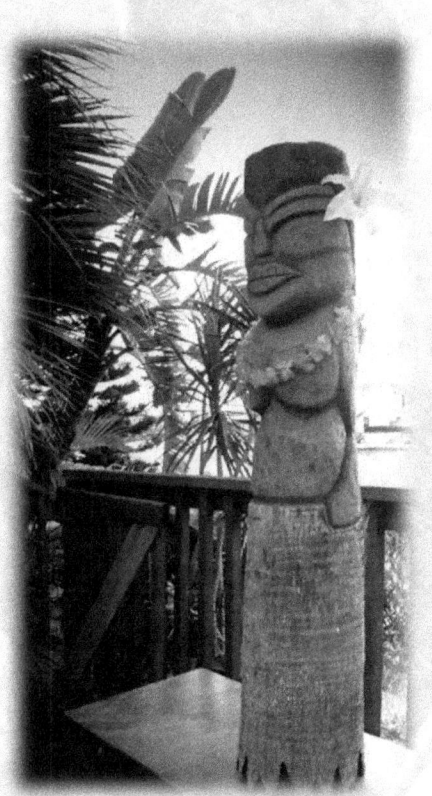

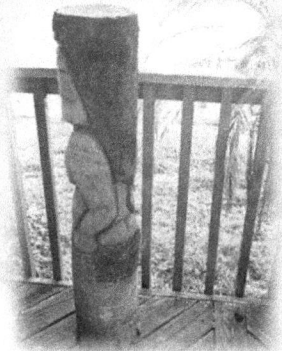

My first attempt was appreciated by one collector, but I had to do better. I had to make something more graceful, and so I put some time into this next one. *I can see her butt crack!*

*Hoaihu comes to man and woman in times of anger. He can appear for a short time from the pestering of a fly or linger for many days from the treachery of a friend. Hoaihu is not a friend. Man must remember the power of Hoaihu to give him strength to survive, or the same to destroy himself when the spirit visits.*

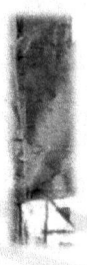

## Girl of the Month Club

I had a hankering for more and more ladies now. I went directly into another female project. This time I created a Maori maiden. She is complete with the traditional chin moko tattoo and tattooing of the lips. Looking back, I would like to have given her more neck. She is particularly chesty to the point of them growing directly from under her chin, but with all her faults, I am still quite taken with her.

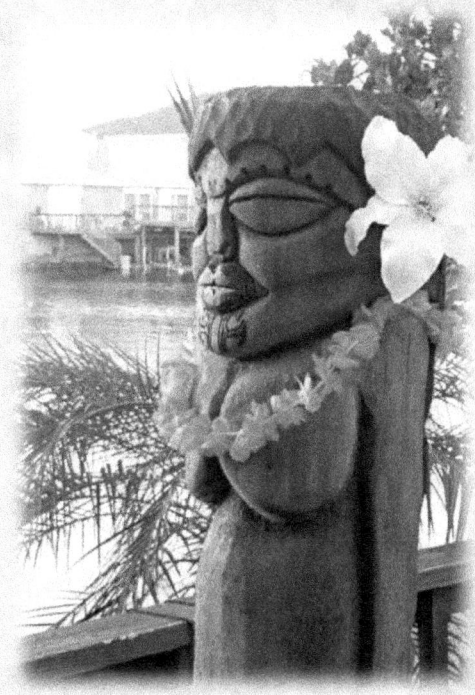

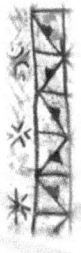

Makamatea is the god of fear. It can take both male and female forms so there is no speaking of Makamatea as either he or she. Like Hoaihu, Makamatea can be very useful to man and woman but can also take control and destroy them, both by foolish action or by cowardice.

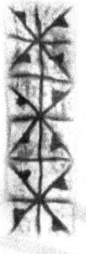

## *Give Them What They Want*

The arsenal for the art walk this year. Two new females, a few leftovers, a chunky Maori with moko, and two low-priced little guys.

There was much praise for the females, but no takers. I may have been too enamored with them and priced them too high. I ended up selling the Maori stump and the two little tikis. Not a roaring success, but that didn't matter. Something amazing was about to happen.

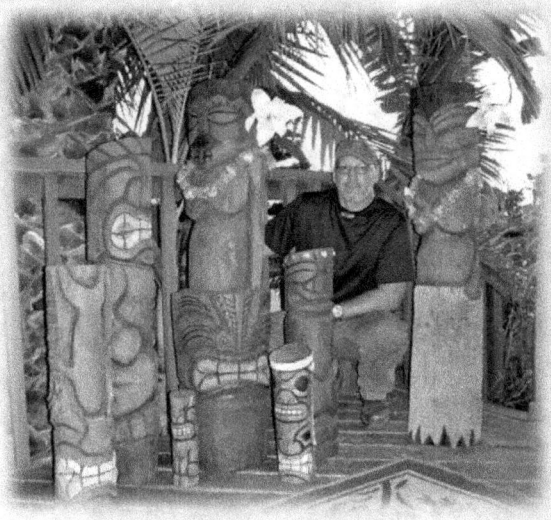

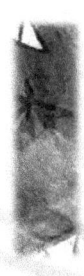

*Vaulofa is the goddess of love. She travels with the wind, in quick gusts or in gentle breezes. In the lifetime of man and woman she may visit quickly or may endure forever. She takes her spirit upon man and woman in different ways and at different times during life. Vaulofa is always welcome, as she may disappear for a time.*

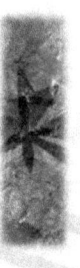

## Giving Out Free Samples

So remember the email from way back? It turns out that it was not from an individual wanting tikis for his backyard project, it was from a business. A very established restaurant right on the island which I live, and a fixture in the community for decades.

They wanted a meeting! The manager showed me an area that was underutilized which they wanted to "tikify". They had existing squared support beams that would have to be carved into, or a flat-back tiki would have to be affixed to them. I left the meeting with a homework assignment. They would like two samples, one of a tiki on a square post sample, and one on a large half-log.

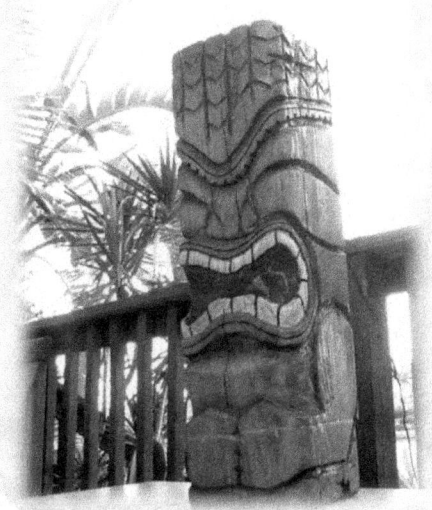

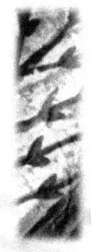

Working in cooperation with Uti, derived from her bounty is Wailamava, the god of spirit drinks and trickery. Waila-mava is a friend and will play tricks with and make sport of the feelings of man and woman. Because of Wailamava's playful nature and trickery, he can draw the ire of all other gods if he reveals himself at improper times, or too often.

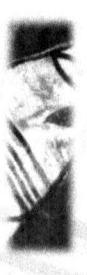

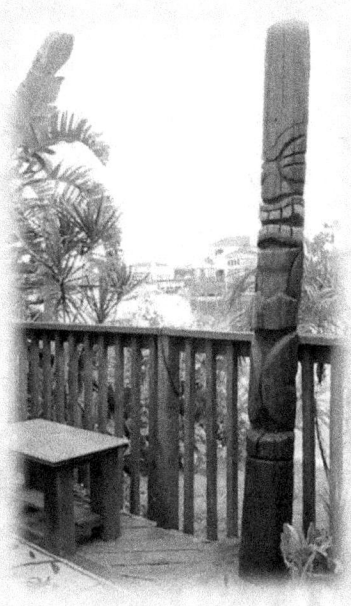

At our next meeting, the samples were very well received. We discussed some project possibilities around the establishment, both immediate plans and possible plans for the future. We ended the meeting with a goal to create tikis around existing support posts at the bar areas, and two grand tiki guards at the entrance. All that was needed from me would be a proposal and a price quote. Can do!

I came up with a design plan and a quote for each piece that I would be working on. I priced it in a way that would be fair to them, but also to me. Thankfully, they were giving me a very reasonable timeline to complete this project. I kept this in mind when putting together the final proposal.

I clicked the send button and waited. It would be less than a couple of hours before receiving the simple response- "Looks good. When can you start?"

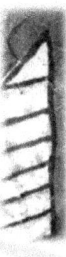

Pumauhi is the god of confusion. When feelings of man or woman mix without direction, they are visited by Pumauhi. He can visit in a deep forest or under the ocean surface. Often without intent, man and woman summon Pumauhi when he schemes together with Wailamava.

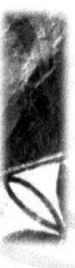

## And so it Begins!

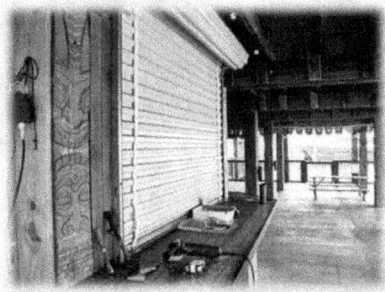

I got started immediately. I invested in some new tools and took photos around the establishment. I studied these and carefully planned my design for each piece. I began sketching the next day, and carving

the day after that. I devoted a couple of hours of carving per day after work, then carved for two half-days on the weekends.

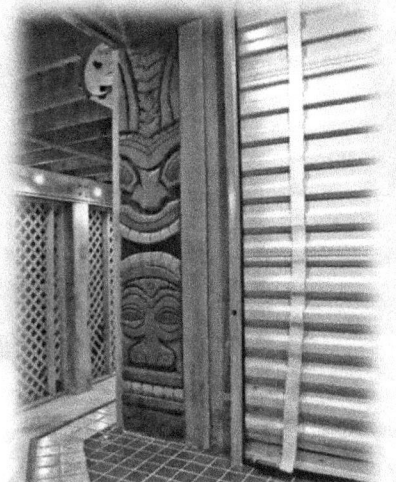

The first piece was a flat tiki on an exposed piece of beam at one side of a bar. This would be the simplest piece of the project, even though I had never carved a flat piece before. No time to start like the first time.

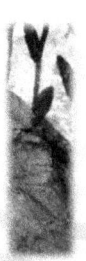

*Tahaihue is the god of thievery and deceit. He takes no earthly shape lest the other gods destroy him, yet he can be hiding and lurking throughout all of the earth, even the oceans. Tahaihue can infect the children of man and woman, and puts at risk the bounty and pleasures of all.*

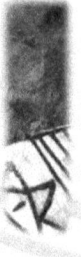

## Their Faces Were Beaming

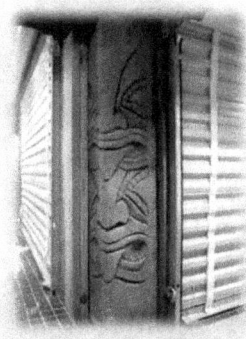

Moving along the bar, another first for me was presented. I would create this piece on the corner of a support beam. This was quite unknown territory for me, but I now am interested in doing more like it in the future as this lent itself to quite a unique look.

This ended up being a Maori-inspired, two-headed tiki complete with hanging tongues of the haka and moko facial tattoos. I received a lot of compliments from observers as I worked on this one and more upon completion. This, along with the first flat-back tiki complimented this portion of the bar and its serving area nicely.

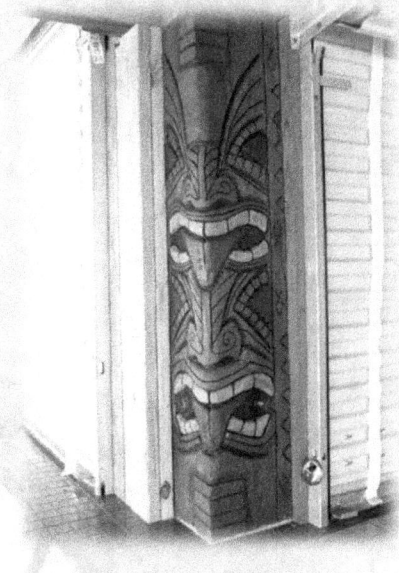

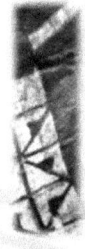

Taroha is the god of all things charitable. Taroha appears in the exchanging of gifts, assistance to others with difficult tasks, and lending of items. When bad luck befalls a family, other families may give aid with food, care of children and helping with chores- all through Taroha's added strength and ideas.

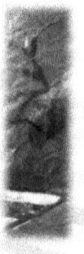

## Phase One Completed

Two tikis are now decorating the secondary bar serving windows. This was a nice warmup for this ambitious project where I learned the ins and outs of working with these existing supports. I now had experience with negotiating my work around the counter areas and creating an appealing look with both cornered and flat wood surfaces.

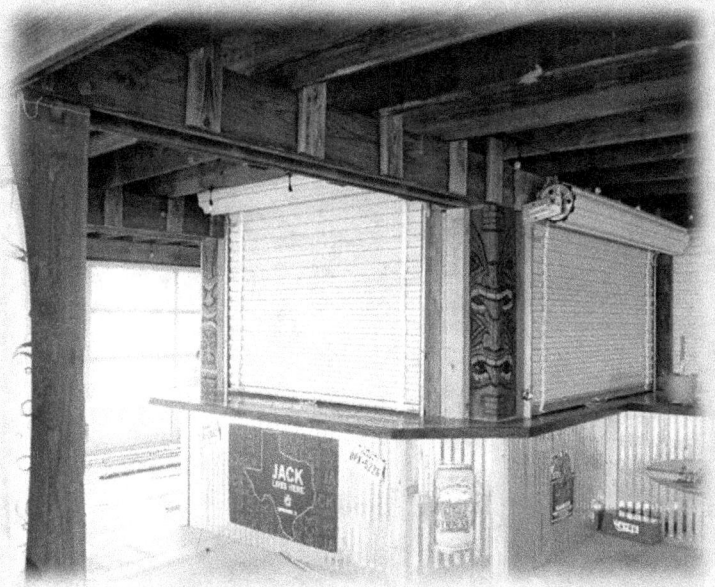

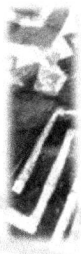

When man and woman of different tribes engage in fighting, they are influenced by Taputaua. Taputaua is the god of war and fighting. All men and women pray to Taputaua for strength at this time. Taputaua gives them this strength reluctantly, as man and woman have made this choice, but shows no favor. Taputaua is feared by all gods but is respected as fair of mind.

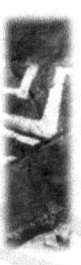

## Not that Tiki Bar, the Other One

The establishment actually has multiple bar areas. This is the main serving area with four feet of exposed support beam in need of transformation. This in addition to three other tikis required in this area.

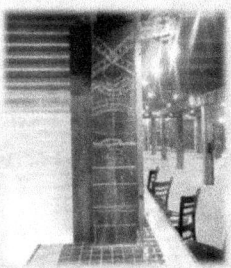
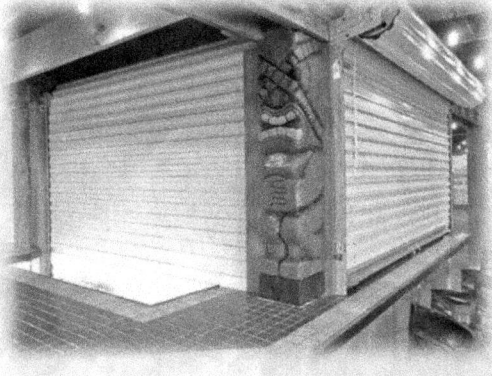

This piece I had mixed feelings about upon completion, but it has grown on me under the correct lighting. My regrets involve the style of eyes I chose, which I have not repeated since, and some mistakes in the cutting of the legs which I alone notice. I do think his folded hands and style of chest have something going for them, along with the facial cross pattern.

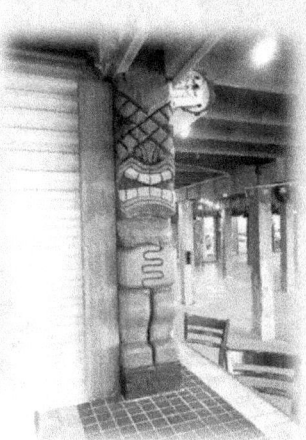

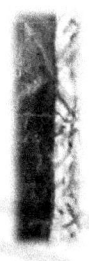

When Taputaua leaves the spirit of man and woman, the graces of Figomalu then cover the earth. Figomalu is the goddess of peace. She is most closely acquainted on earth through grandmothers, who most often reveal her way. Figomalu works closely with Niu, Talo, Heimoa, Sahonu, Puavao, Falea'efe, Uti- all gods of sustenance, always working to make deals and efforts for peace. As with Taputaua, she is respected by all gods equally.

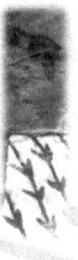

## He Hasn't Been Showing Up for Work

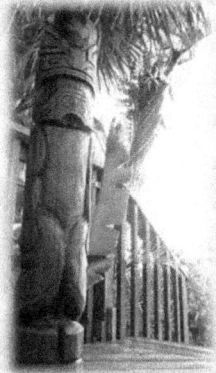

This piece was done off site at my home. Using one quarter of the flat-back half-log from the sample I created for this project, it was cut in half yet again for this tiki. This was bolted into the bar and the bolt heads counter sunk, puttied, and stained over to match the tiki's coloration. The shape of the great state of Texas graces this warrior's forehead.

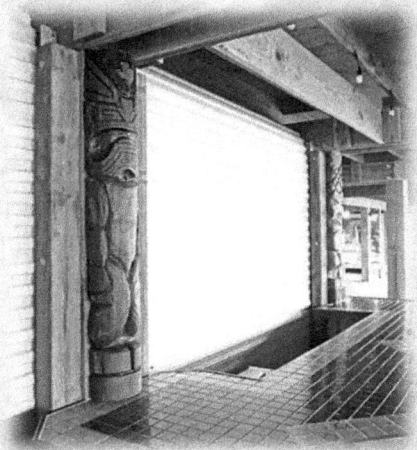

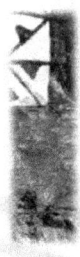

*Ilitukupolo is both a god and a place. It is the under-world. A place of despair and the only place where Tahaihue takes his wretched shape and many times over. Rejected by other gods, Ilitukupolo rules here, while the infinite twins of Tahaihue do his bidding in tormenting all that may find themselves in his domain.*

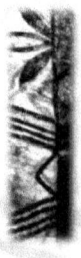

## Taking Things in for a Moment

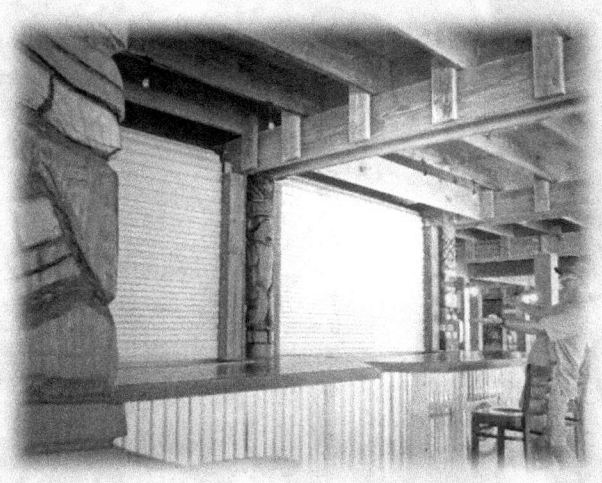

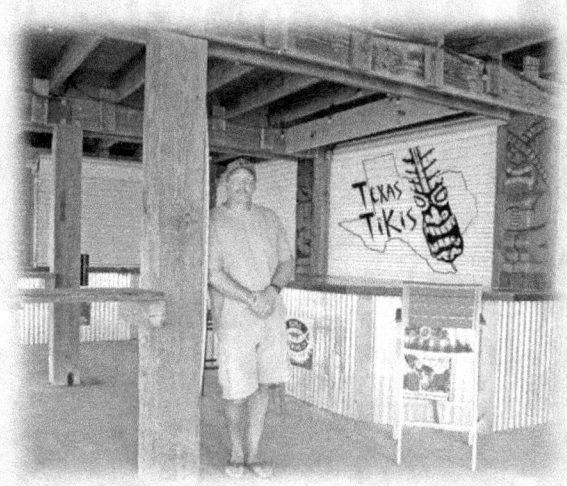

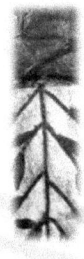

Lara'i is the other side to Ilitukupolo in the land of heaven. Man and woman come here at completion of their time of earth if their time was that of deference to all gods. The bounties of the earth and times of the spirit of Figomalu are multiplied here by one thousand. Lara'i has room for all good ancestors of man and woman in her home, and with no change in time.

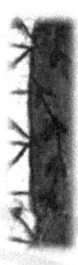

## Eight Feet of Awesome

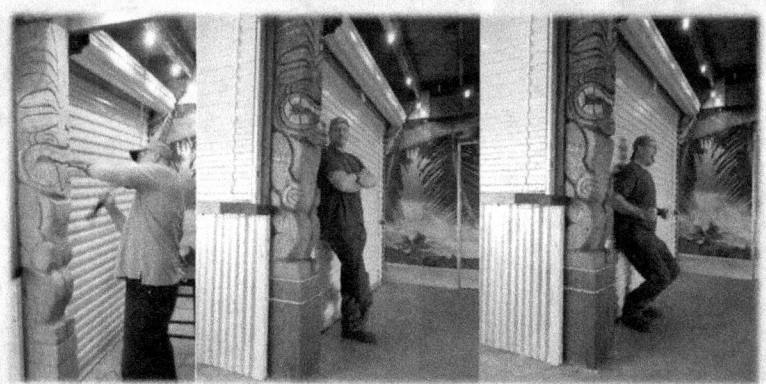

An eight foot beam supports the opposite side of the primary bar area. I had three sides of beam to carve on from floor to ceiling. The eyes, nose and hands are inspired by tikis of the Marquesan islands. A Samoan style tattoo graces this warrior's right arm.

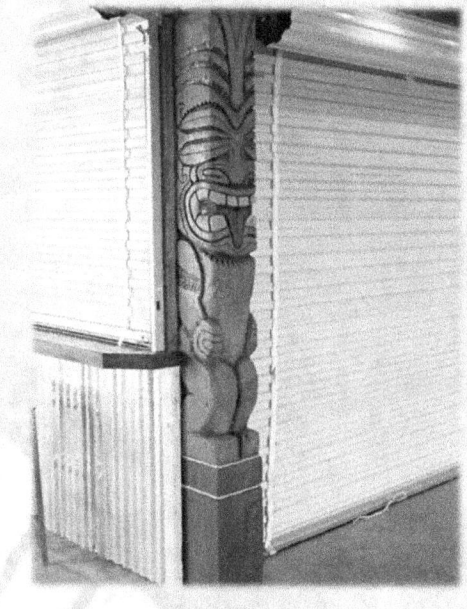

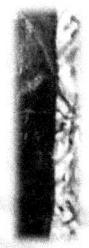

Falea'efe provided a new proposal to the moon. "We have given man and woman so much for help on this earth!" he said. "This is so" said the moon. "But I would like yet another tool provided to our beings. That they may make change to such hazards that may confound them, and improve the earth for themselves."

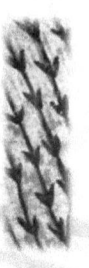

## Guarding the Entrance

The final creations of this project would have to be bold, strong, and deliver an unmistakable effect. These are the two

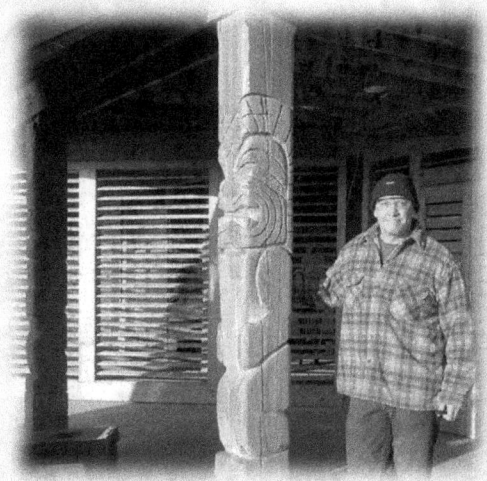

tiki warriors that guard the front entrance. A statement to all who wish to enter. They welcome all who are of good will. Those with evil intent, however, enter at their own peril.

I first proposed that I make them identical twins. I later was given permission to make them slightly different in style. Both would still sit at the same height, on identical pedestals and both share the same proportions. Each are well over eight feet in height.

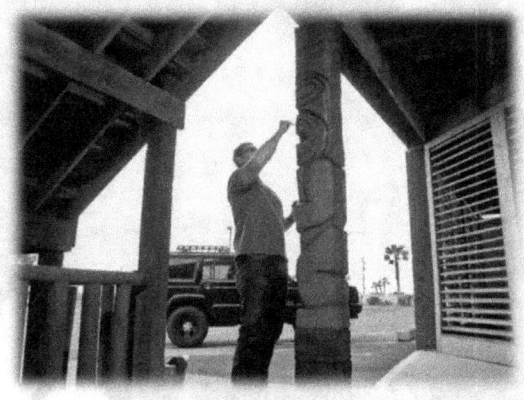

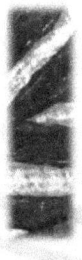

"On this we agree." said the Moon, "So what do you suggest?" Falea'efe then created Tiaoako, the god of learning. Tiaoako guides man and woman through problems and presents himself in ideas, experimentation and that which teaches children proper ways on earth.

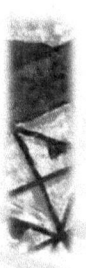

## Public Exposure

An unfortunate obstacle to making the most dramatic statement by my tikis at the establishment's entrance was this large staircase. It is positioned so that both tikis are difficult to view at the same time when walking in. On the way out, however, female patrons can enjoy the buttocks of these two proud posers.

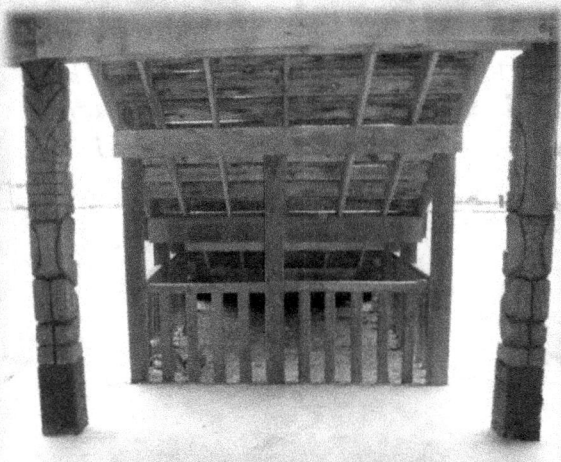

*Two bare wooden backsides*

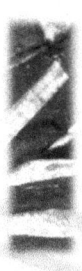

The moon said to Falea'efe "I too would like to add yet another god of the mind for man and woman" he announced. "Of what sort?" Falea'efe asked. "When I appear at night, man and woman quickly leave from me. Sometimes they may look up, but they are quickly gone. I cannot see nor care for them at night, but I may still give them light."

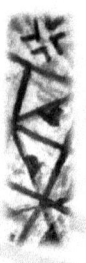

## Tiki Bouncers on Duty

Here we have the two completed warrior guards. These are exposed to the elements at all times, but checking on them a year later I found the deck stain to be holding up nicely and both pieces looking just as I left them, even after a category four hurricane.

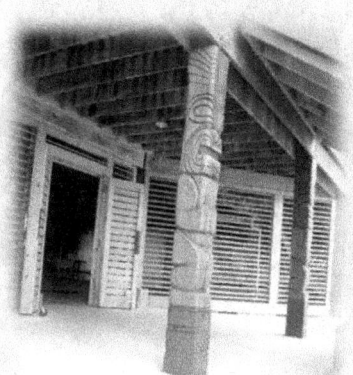
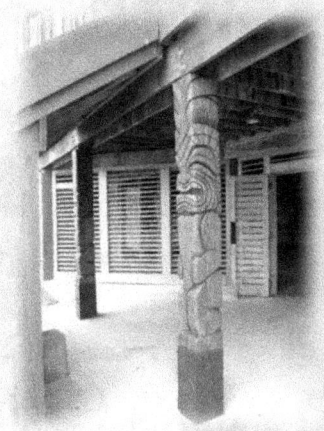
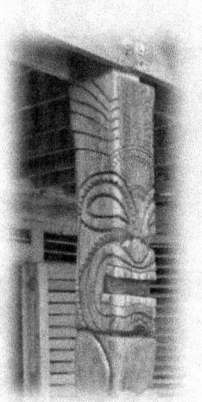
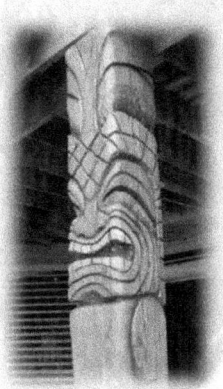
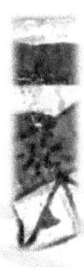

And so the moon created the god Mouami'i. At night Mouami'i visits man and woman, she is the goddess of dreams. She creates stories and ideas as man and woman rest. She gives them contact with those that they love and those that have gone on to Lara'i.

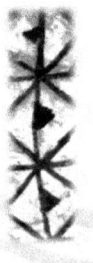

## Continuing the Routine

Things settled down a great deal after the custom bar project. In fact, things died off all together. This became an excuse to take a week or two off and address some household projects that had been put off for a while.

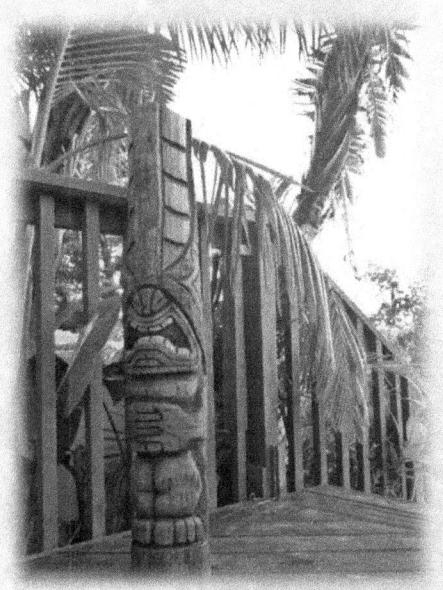

The tiki spirit returned soon enough however, and I had the raw logs to do something about it. I decided that now would be a good time to pursue some

new styles that I had not touched on. For so long I had been inspired by the outer reaches of Polynesia, that I had com-

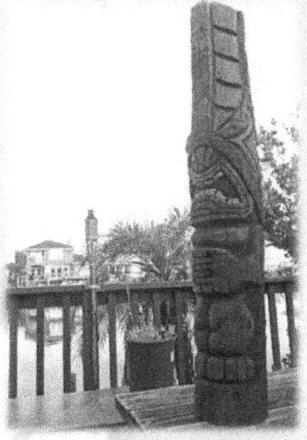

pletely forgotten about the traditional Hawaiian-inspired styles.

I decided to give this a go and went in the direction of Lono, god of fertility. This to me meant a high headdress and pronounced lower lip. I would, of course, put my own spin on things and came up with this palm, Lono-inspired piece.

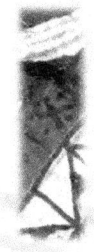

The moon and Falea'efe became tired. "We have created much for man and woman" said the moon. "Agreed" replied Falea'efe, "Perhaps it can now be time for man and woman themselves to create." "Too be sure" agreed the moon, "I see much of the earth from above, yet sadly, there is much that I may miss or cannot see."

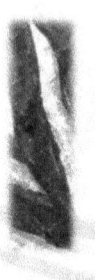

## Dos Lonos

I liked the way this new attempt worked out for me. I went directly into a tiki of similar Lono look for my next project. This time it would be larger, five feet tall in fact.

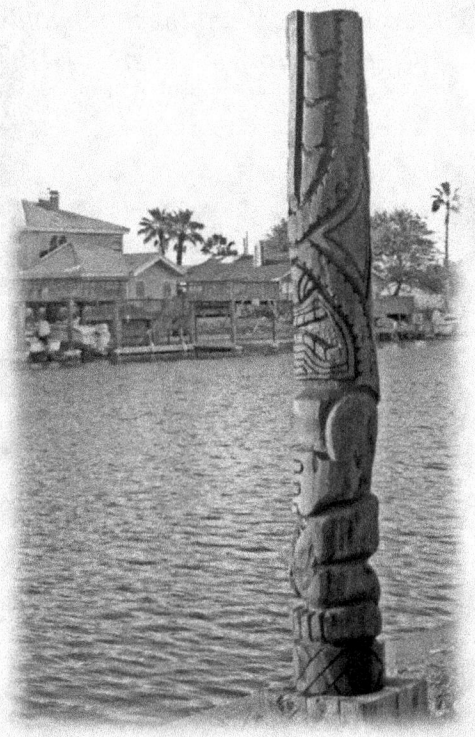

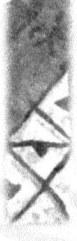

*"It must be put upon man and woman that their lives may become stories. It must be they that relay these stories to their children and others." Cooperating together, the moon and Falea'efe created Rarufa'a, the god of stories and storytelling.*

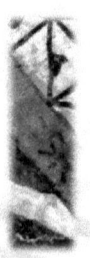

## Still Plugging Along

And so the annual ritual continues with this latest batch of tikis for the year's end. New experiences were had and new styles were dabbled in. The only thing left to do now is move on to whatever comes next and explore uncharted ideas.

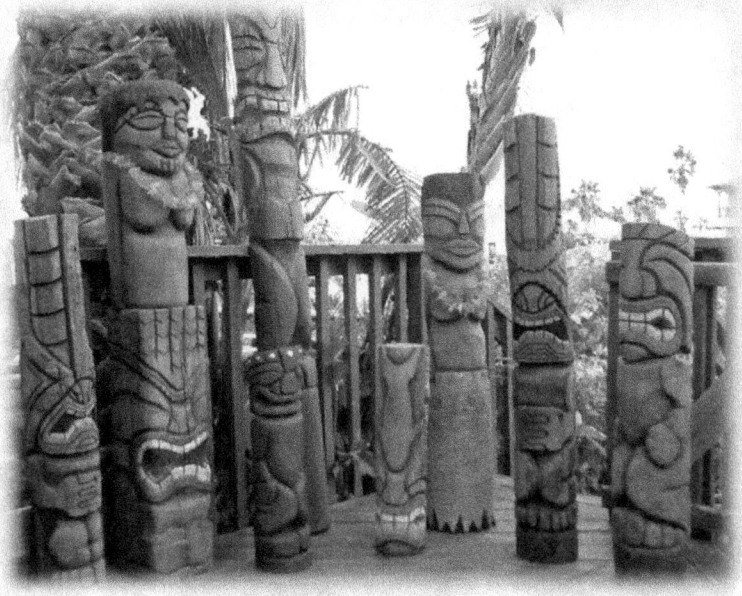

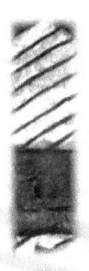

*Rarufa'a works through the man that has much to say. He is evident in the man that makes words that capture the attention of the village. At night this man is filled with the spirit of Rarufa'a- his gestures, his tone, and his memory are unrivalled as he conveys information to all that sit at the fire.*

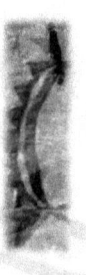

## Wood is but Temporary

I can account for the early demise of a tiki carving when I place blame on my selection of an inferior piece of wood, as in this example eaten by termites, and reluctantly discarded in a mountain community rubbish pile.

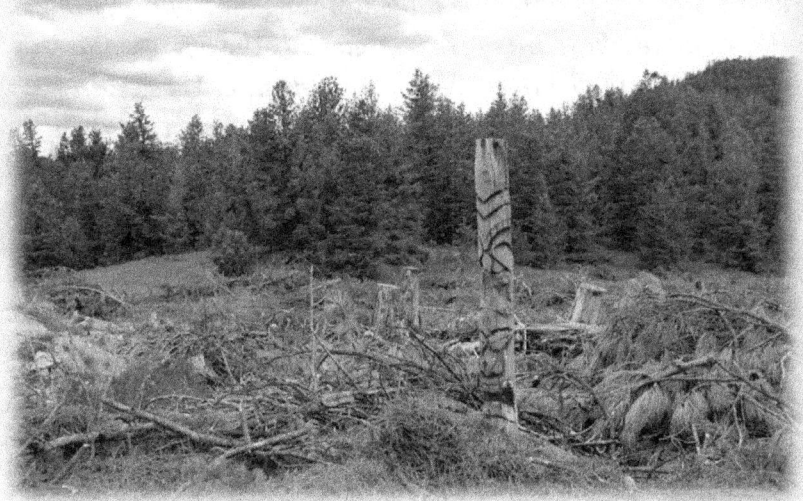

*Photo by Michael Hockmuller*

This was never intended to be a serious piece made for anyone in particular, just a quick diversion during a Colorado vacation. It did provide some lessons though. I have control over the quality of the medium, and most of my tikis will last through my lifetime if I carefully think this through.

*These things I create have a lifespan. Although wood carvings exist that are hundreds of years old, most that were created by the early Polynesians are long gone now. Mine will no doubt share this fate in time, but the energy and inspiration channeled into them will continue. These will swirl around through the soil, water, and air of the earth, eventually landing on the shoulder of some other creator.*

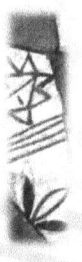

# Mark Ferdinand

Mark Ferdinand lives on the South Texas coast with his wife, daughter and son. Fishing the surf, hunting, gardening, tiki carving, and DIY projects occupy his spare time. He has written on the topic of autism spectrum disorder from a father's perspective in parenting articles and in fiction. Mark has also written on his experiences with working with venomous snakes and other creatures.

# Books by Mark Ferdinand

- *Autism and Fatherhood*

- *Fortune on the Spectrum –
  An Adventure Novel*

- *You're Gonna' Get Bit! –
  Harrowing Tales of Herpetology*

- *The Autistic Prankster –
  Enjoying the Fun Side of Autism*

- *Every Tiki has a Spirit*

- *Bachelor on the Spectrum
  (Coming Soon!)*

Beyond paperback Mark's books can be
purchased for Kindle, Android, and Apple devices.

*EVERY TIKI HAS A SPIRIT*

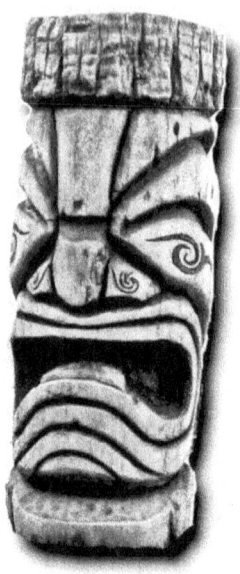

EVERY TIKI HAS A SPIRIT

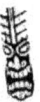